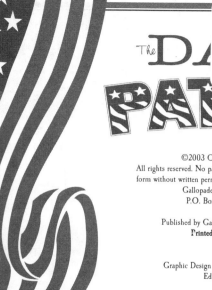

The **D**...

PAT RIOT

Published by Gallopade International/Carole Marsh Books.
Printed in the United States of America!

Edited by Carole Marsh
Graphic Design and Editorial Assistant: Steven St. Laurent
Editorial Assistant: Rachel Moss

This book is typeset in Caslon Antique.
The first press-printing of the Declaration of Independence
was typeset—at Benjamin Franklin's request—in Caslon.

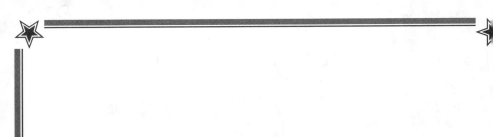

for Boom Pa,
with love

My country 'tis of thee,
Sweet land of liberty,
Of thee I sing;
Land where my father died,
Land of the pilgrim's pride,
From every mountain side
Let freedom ring.

—Samuel Francis Smith, *America*

1

I hear America singing, the varied carols I hear.

—Walt Whitman, *Leaves of Grass*, "I Hear America Singing"

2

It was wonderful to find America, but it would
have been more wonderful to miss it.

—Mark Twain, *Pudd'nhead Wilson's Calender*

3

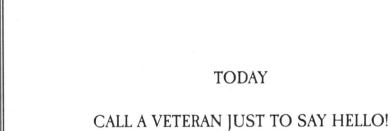

TODAY

CALL A VETERAN JUST TO SAY HELLO!

The youth of America is their oldest tradition.
It has been going on now for three hundred years.

–Oscar Wilde, *A Woman of No Importance*

5

Our whole duty, for the present at any rate, is summed up in
the motto: America first.

—President Woodrow Wilson, from
a speech in New York, April 20, 1915

O beautiful for spacious skies,
For amber waves of grain,
For purple mountain majesties
Above the fruited plain!
America! America!
God shed his grace on thee
And crown thy good with brotherhood
From sea to shining sea!

—Katharine Lee Bates, *America the Beautiful*

TODAY

READ A BOOK ON AMERICAN HISTORY,
THEN PASS IT ALONG TO A TEENAGER!

8

American life is a powerful solvent. It seems to neutralise
every intellectual element, however tough and alien it may be,
and to fuse it in the native good-will, complacency,
thoughtlessness, and optimism.

—James Harvey Robinson, *Character and Opinion in the
United States*

Providence, that watches over children, drunkards,
and fools with silent miracles and other esoterica,
continue to suspend the ordinary rules and take
care of the United States of America.

—Arthur Guiterman, *Gaily the Troubadour*

TODAY

BAKE A CAKE (OR BUY ONE)
AND TAKE IT TO A VETERAN'S HOME!

11

A sound American is simply one who has put out of his mind all doubts and questionings, and who accepts instantly, and as incontrovertible gospel, the whole body of official doctrine of his day, whatever it may be and no matter how often it may change. The instant he challenges it, no matter how timorously and academically, he ceases by that much to be a loyal and creditable citizen of the Republic.

–H. L. Mencken in the *Baltimore Evening Sun*, March 12, 1923

Every third American devotes himself to improving and uplifting his fellow citizens, usually by force.

—H. L. Mencken, *Prejudices: First Series*

There are no second acts in American lives.

—F. Scott Fitzgerald, *The Last Tycoon*

TODAY

BE SURE YOU ARE REGISTERED TO VOTE,
PUT THE NEXT VOTING DATE ON
YOUR CALENDAR, AND ENCOURAGE
A NON-VOTER TO VOTE!

A glorious death is his
Who for his country falls.

—Homer, *Illiad* XV

It is sweet and proper to die for the fatherland.

—Horace, *Odes* III.ii.

17

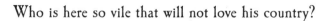

Who is here so vile that will not love his country?

—Shakespeare, *Julius Caesar* III.ii.

What pity is it that we can die but once to serve our country!

—Joseph Addison, *Cato* IV

TODAY

EXPLAIN TO A CHILD WHAT PATRIOTISM MEANS!

Patriotism is the last refuge of a scoundrel.

—Samuel Johnson in Boswell's *Life*, April 7, 1775

21

I only regret that I have but one life to lose for my country.

—Nathan Hale, his last words, September 22, 1776

22

Then conquer we must, for our cause is just,
And this be our motto: "In God we trust!"
And the star-spangled banner in triumph shall wave,
O'er the land of the free, and the home of the brave!

—Francis Scott Key, *The Star-Spangled Banner*

Breathes there the man, with soul so dead,
Who never to himself hath said,
This is my own, my native land!
Whose heart hath ne'er within him burn'd,
As home his footsteps he hath turn'd,
From wandering on a foreign strand!
If such there breathe, go, mark him well;
For him no minstrel raptures swell;
High though his titles, proud his name;
Boundless his wealth as wish can claim—
Despite those titles, power, and pelf,
The wretch, concentred all in self,
Living, shall forfeit fair renown,
And, doubly dying, shall go down
To the vile dust, from whence he sprung,
Unwept, unhonour'd, and unsung.

—Sir Walter Scott, *The Lay of the Last Minstrel* VI

TODAY

LEARN ALL THE WORDS TO ALL THOSE PATRIOTIC SONGS!

The Beautiful, the Sacred—
Which, in all climes, men that have hearts
adore by the great title of their mother country!

—E. G. Bulwer-Lytton, *Richelieu* IV.ii.

Patriotism is a kind of religion;
it is the egg from which wars are hatched.

—Guy de Maupassant, *My Uncle Sosthenes*

That pernicious sentiment, "Our country, right or wrong."

—James Russell Lowell, *The Biglow Papers* I.iii.

Let not Avarice quench the fire,
That patriotism should inspire;
With general voice exclaim:
"Away all sordid thoughts of greater pay."

—*Chamber's Journal*, October 1854

TODAY

TELL SOMEONE WHAT
FREEDOM
MEANS TO YOU!

You'll never have a quiet world till you knock the patriotism
out of the human race.

–G. B. Shaw, *O'Flaherty, V.C.*

Originality and initiative are what I ask for my country.

—Robert Frost, *The Figure a Poem Makes*

One of the greatest attractions of patriotism—it fulfills our worst wishes. In the person of our nation we are able, vicariously, to bully and cheat. Bully and cheat, what's more, with a feeling that we are profoundly virtuous.

—Aldous Huxley, *Eyeless in Gaza*, chapter XVII

Ask not what your country can do for you;
ask what you can do for your country.

—John F. Kennedy, Inaugural Address, 1961

Is not a Patron, my Lord, one who looks
with unconcern on a man struggling for life in the water,
and, when he has reached ground,
encumbers him with help?

—Samuel Johnson, Letter to the Earl
of Chesterfield, Feb. 7, 1775

TODAY

CONGRATULATE AND THANK
A RETURNING VETERAN!

Let every nation know, whether it wishes us well or ill,
that we will pay any price,
bear any burden,
meet any hardship,
support any friend,
oppose any foe,
in order to assure the survival and the success of liberty.

—President John F. Kennedy,
Inaugural Address, January 20, 1961

Only our individual faith in freedom can keep us free.

—President Dwight D. Eisenhower

A nation which makes the final sacrifice
for life and freedom does not get beaten.

—Kemal Ataturk

Liberty is to the collective body,
what health is to every individual body.
Without health no pleasure can be tasted by man;
without liberty,
no happiness can be enjoyed by society.

—Henry Bolingbroke

TODAY

HELP A CHILD WRITE OUT
A DEFINITION OF PATRIOTISM!

All the great things are simple,
and many can be expressed in a single word:
freedom;
justice;
honor;
duty;
mercy;
hope.

—Sir Winston Churchill

In the long history of the world,
only a few generations have been granted
the role of defending freedom in its hour
of maximum danger.
I do not shrink from this responsibility—I welcome it.

—President John F. Kennedy

43

Freedom is the last, best hope of earth.

—President Abraham Lincoln

Those who expect to reap the blessings of freedom must,
like men, undergo the fatigue of supporting it.

—Thomas Paine

TODAY

FIND THAT FLAG PIN AND PUT IT
ON YOUR LAPEL!

Freedom of opinion can only exist
when the government thinks itself secure.

—Bertrand Russell

Freedom exists only with power.

—Johann Friedrich Von Schiller

I know not what course others may take,
but as for me, give me liberty or give me death.

—Patrick Henry

To sin by silence when they should protest
makes cowards of men.

—President Abraham Lincoln

TODAY

BE A PATRIOT—
PICK UP LITTER YOU DIDN'T DROP!

They that can give up essential liberty to obtain a little
temporary safety deserve neither liberty nor safety.

—Benjamin Franklin

"My country, right or wrong" is a thing that no patriot
would think of saying except in a desperate case.
It is like saying "My mother, drunk or sober."

Gilbert Keith Chesterton, in *Defence of Patriotism*

A house divided against itself cannot stand.

—President Abraham Lincoln

TODAY

WEAR RED, WHITE, AND BLUE!

The battle, sir, is not to the strong alone;
it is to the vigilant, the active, the brave.

—Patrick Henry, March 23, 1775

America will never be destroyed from the outside.
If we falter and lose our freedoms,
it will be because we destroyed ourselves.

—President Abraham Lincoln

Character is doing the right thing when no one is watching.

–J. C. Watts

The basis of a democratic state is liberty.

—Aristotle

TODAY

READ THE U.S. CONSTITUTION!

60

Injustice anywhere is a threat to justice everywhere.

—Martin Luther King, Jr.

Patriotism is an intricate combination of love
for one's country, family and fellow man.
It is a different feeling for every individual,
yet it is the inexplicable bond that unites us as Americans.

—President Jimmy Carter

Now more than ever we need to honor our principles
of freedom, democracy and human rights
and the sacrifices made by those who
established and have preserved these blessings in America.

—Former U.S. Senator Sam Nunn

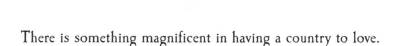

There is something magnificent in having a country to love.

—James Russell Lowell

I shall know but one country.
The ends I aim at shall be my country's,
my God's and Truth's.
I was born an American;
I live as an American;
I shall die as an American.

—Daniel Webster

TODAY

READ THE BILL OF RIGHTS
TO A CLASSROOM FULL OF KIDS!

Sometimes people call me an idealist.
Well, that is the way I know I am an American.
America is the only idealistic nation in the world.

—President Woodrow Wilson

We go forth all to seek America.
And in the seeking we create her.
In the quality of our search shall be the nature
of the American that we created.

—Waldo Frank

The independence and liberty you possess
are the work of joint efforts, of common dangers,
sufferings, and successes.

—President George Washington

One country, one constitution, one destiny.

—Daniel Webster

TODAY

VISIT THE NATIONAL D-DAY MUSEUM,
OR MAKE PLANS TO!
IN THE MEANTIME, VISIT THEIR WEBSITE!

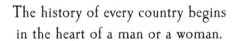

The history of every country begins
in the heart of a man or a woman.

–Willa Cather

72

America was established not to create wealth
but to realize a vision, to realize an ideal—
to discover and maintain liberty among men.

—President Woodrow Wilson

Driven from every other corner of the earth,
freedom of thought and the right of private judgment
in matters of conscience direct their course
to this happy country as their last asylum.

—Samuel Adams

TODAY

MAKE A DONATION TO THE NEW NATIONAL MUSEUM OF PATRIOTISM THAT WILL OPEN IN ATLANTA, GEORGIA IN 2004!

Great has been the Greek, the Latin, the Slav, The Celts,
the Teuton, and the Anglo-Saxon, but greater than any
of these is the American,
in which are blended the virtues of them all.

—William Jennings Bryan

What constitutes an American? Not color nor race nor religion. Not the pedigree of his family nor the place of his birth. Not the coincidence of his citizenship. An American is one who loves justice and believes in the dignity of man. An American is one who will fight for his freedom and that of his neighbor. An American is one who will sacrifice property, ease, and security in order that he and his children may retain the rights of all free men.

—Harold Ickes, "I Am an American" speech

77

The whole history of our continent is a history of the imagination. Men imagined land beyond the sea and found it. Men imagined the forests, the great plains, the rivers, the mountains—and found these plains and mountains. They came, as the great explorers crossed the Atlantic, because of the imagination of their minds—because they imagined a better, a more beautiful, a freer, happier world.

—Archibald Macleish

78

TODAY

TAKE TIME TO SHARE A MEMORY
WITH A VETERAN!

America is a passionate idea or it is nothing.
America is a human brotherhood or it is chaos.

—Max Lerner

America lives in the heart of every man everywhere
who wishes to find a region where he will be free
to work out his destiny as he chooses.

—President Woodrow Wilson

God has a divine purpose in placing this land
between two great oceans to be found by those
who had a special love of freedom and courage.

—President Ronald Reagan

The happy ending is our national belief.

−Mary McCarthy

TODAY

SING THE NATIONAL ANTHEM
(EVEN IF THERE IS NO BALL GAME!).

One flag, one land, one heart, one hand,
One Nation, evermore!

—Oliver Wendell Holmes

The American, by nature, is optimistic.
He is experimental, an inventor and a builder
who builds best when called upon to build greatly.

—President John F. Kennedy

We are a nation of many nationalities,
many races, many religions—
bound together by a single unity,
the unity of freedom and equality.

—President Franklin D. Roosevelt

America—The place where miracles not only happen,
but where they happen all the time.

—Thomas Wolfe

There is no "Republican," no "Democrat,"
on the Fourth of July—all are Americans.
All feel that their country is greater than party.

—James Gillespie

We are not so much a nation as a world.

—Herman Melville

TODAY

WRITE A LETTER TO THE EDITOR;
SAY SOMETHING PATRIOTIC AND POSITIVE!

There is no security on earth; there is only opportunity.

—General Douglas MacArthur

The greater part of our happiness or misery depends on our disposition, and not our circumstances.

—First First Lady Martha Washington

The U.S. Constitution doesn't guarantee happiness,
only the pursuit of it.
You have to catch up with it yourself.

—Benjamin Franklin

With all its faults, the American political system
is the freest and most democratic in the world.

—Eldridge Cleaver

TODAY

SAY THE PLEDGE OF ALLEGIANCE,
EVEN IF IT'S TO YOURSELF!

Man's capacity for evil makes democracy necessary,
and man's capacity for good makes democracy possible.

—Reinhold Niebuhr

Generosity is the flower of justice.

—Nathaniel Hawthorne

The American is wonderfully alive; and his vitality, not having often found a suitable outlet, makes him appear agitated on the surface; he is always letting off an unnecessarily loud blast of incidental steam. Yet his vitality is not superficial; it is inwardly prompted, and as sensitive and quick as a magnetic needle. He is inquisitive, and ready with an answer to any question that he may put himself of his own accord; but if you try to pour instruction into him, on matters that do not touch his own spontaneous life, he shows the most extraordinary powers of resistance and oblivescence; so that he often is remarkably expert in some directions and surprisingly obtuse in others. He seems to bear lightly the sorrowful burden of human knowledge. In a word, he is young.

—George Santayana

99

A peaceful world is a world in which differences
are tolerated, and are not eliminated by violence.

—John Foster Dulles

TODAY

WEAR A POPPY . . .
AND KNOW WHY YOU ARE WEARING IT!

Sure I wave the American flag.
Do you know a better flag to wave?
Sure I love my country with all her faults.
I'm not ashamed of that,
never have been, never will be.

—John Wayne

The real and lasting victories
are those of peace and not of war.

—Ralph Waldo Emerson

In this unconquerably and justifiably optimistic nation
nothing undertaken by free men and
free women is impossible.

—Robert E. Sherwood

TODAY

LEARN THE NAMES OF SOME OF THOSE
SOUTH PACIFIC ISLANDS–
OUR BOYS DIED THERE!

War is an ugly thing, but not the ugliest of things.
The decayed and degraded state of moral patriotic feeling
which thinks that nothing is worth war is much worse.
The person who has nothing for which he is willing to fight,
nothing which is more important than his own personal safety,
is a miserable creature, and has no chance of being free unless
made or kept so by the exertions of better men than himself.

—John Stuart Mill

Throughout history it has been the inaction of those who could have acted, the indifference of those who should have known better, the silence of the voice of justice when it mattered most, that has made it possible for evil to triumph.

—Haile Selassie

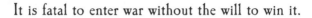

It is fatal to enter war without the will to win it.

—General Douglas MacArthur

Older men declare war.
But it is the youth that must fight and die.

—President Herbert Hoover

The purpose of all war is ultimately peace.

–Saint Augustine

TODAY

TEACH A KID HOW TO SALUTE A SOLDIER!

111

A good plan today is better than a perfect plan tomorrow.

–General George S. Patton

If everyone is thinking alike, then somebody isn't thinking.

—General George S. Patton

113

If a man does his best, what else is there?

—General George S. Patton

TODAY

HUG A VETERAN,
A RETURNING SOLDIER,
OR SOMEONE WAITING FOR ONE!

I don't measure a man's success by how high he climbs,
but how high he bounces when he hits the bottom.

—General George S. Patton

TODAY
BAKE A PIE OR BUY ONE AND DELIVER
IT TO A VET IN A NURSING HOME!
THEN TAKE TIME TO EAT A PIECE
WITH HIM OR HER!

In forty hours I shall be in battle; with little information;
and on the spur of the moment will have to make
the most momentous decisions;
But I believe that one's spirit enlarges
with responsibility and that, with God's help,
I shall make them and make them right.

—General George S. Patton

118

Patriotism is the willingness to kill
and be killed for trivial reasons.

—Bertrand Russell

America is a great country. It has many shortcomings, many social inequalities, and it's tragic that the problem of the blacks wasn't solved fifty or even a hundred years ago, but it's still a great country, a country full of opportunities, of freedom! Does it seem nothing to you to be able to say what you like, even against the government, the Establishment?

Golda Meir, former Israeli prime minister

120

If there must be trouble let it be in my day,
that my child may have peace.

—Thomas Paine

TODAY

MEMORIZE AT LEAST ONE PATRIOTIC QUOTATION AND SAY IT TO SOMEONE!

When you see a rattlesnake poised to strike,
you do not wait until he has struck before you crush him.

—President Franklin D. Roosevelt

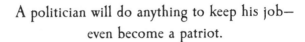

A politician will do anything to keep his job—
even become a patriot.

—William Randolph Hearst

Patriotism is easy to understand in America;
it means looking out for yourself by looking out
for your country.

—President Calvin Coolidge

125

I think patriotism is like charity—it begins at home.

—Henry James

TODAY

LEARN FLAG ETIQUETTE
OR TEACH SOMEONE ELSE!

A man's country is not a certain area of land,
of mountains, rivers, and woods, but it is a principle;
and patriotism is loyalty to that principle.

—George William Curtis

A man's feet must be planted in his country,
but his eyes should survey the world.

—George Santayana

Patriotism is your conviction that this country is superior
to all other countries because you were born in it.

—George Bernard Shaw

130

A thoughtful mind, when it sees a Nation's flag,
sees not the flag only, but the Nation itself,
and whatever may be its symbols, its insignia,
he reads chiefly in the flag the Government,
the principles, the truths, the history which
belongs to the Nation that sets it forth.

—Henry Ward Beecher

131

TODAY

TIE A YELLOW RIBBON
'ROUND AN OLD OAK TREE
(OR AT LEAST YOUR MAILBOX!).

If a man does not keep pace with his companions,
perhaps it is because he hears a different drummer.
Let him step to the music which he hears,
however measured or far away.

—Henry David Thoreau

133

Each man must for himself alone decide what is right
and what is wrong, which course is patriotic and which isn't.
You cannot shirk this and be a man.

—Thomas Tusser

Patriotism is not short, frenzied outbursts of emotion,
but the tranquil and steady dedication of a lifetime.

–Adlai Stevenson

TODAY

GO TO WORK AND DON'T COMPLAIN ABOUT IT—THAT'S PATRIOTISM, TOO!

True patriotism hates injustice in its own land
more than anywhere else.

—Clarence Darrow

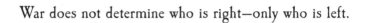

War does not determine who is right—only who is left.

—Anonymous

When war enters a country
It produces lies like sand.

—Anonymous

TODAY

GIVE A LITTLE KID A LITTLE FLAG!

War would end if the dead could return.

–Stanley Baldwin

In time of war the first casualty is truth.

—Boake Carter

War is mainly a catalogue of blunders.

—Winston Churchill

In war, as in life, it is often necessary,
when some cherished scheme has failed,
to take up the best alternative open,
and if so, it is folly not to work for it with all your might.

—Winston Churchill

144

TODAY

PLAN A FLOAT FOR THE NEXT PARADE!

. . . That this nation, under God,
shall have a new birth of freedom,
and that Government of the people, by the people,
for the people, shall not perish from the earth.

—President Abraham Lincoln, Gettysburg Address

Human nature will not change.
In any future great national trial,
compared with the men of this,
we shall have as weak and as strong,
as silly and as wise,
as bad and as good.

—President Abraham Lincoln

147

With malice toward none; with charity for all; with firmness in the right, as God gives us to see the right, let us strive on to finish the work we are in; to bind up the nation's wounds; to care for him who shall have born the battle, and for his widow and his orphan - to do all which may achieve and cherish a just and lasting peace amongst ourselves and with all nations.

—President Abraham Lincoln, Second Inaugural Address

We hold these truths to be self-evident,
that all men are created equal,
that they are endowed by their Creator
with certain unalienable Rights,
that among these are
Life, Liberty, and the pursuit of Happiness.

—Thomas Jefferson,
The Declaration of Independence,
July 4, 1776

TODAY

PAT A VETERAN ON THE BACK AND SAY, "THANKS!"

Four score and seven years ago
our fathers brought forth on this continent a new nation,
conceived in liberty, and dedicated to the proposition
that all men are created equal.

—President Abraham Lincoln

In a chariot of light from the region of the day,
The Goddess of Liberty came
She brought in her hand as
a pledge of her love,
the plant she named Liberty Tree.

—Thomas Paine

What then is the American, this new man? . . . He is an American, who, leaving behind him all his ancient prejudices and manners, receives new ones from the new mode of life he has embraced, the new government he obeys, and the new rank he holds. He becomes an American by being received in the broad lap of our great Alma Mater. Here individuals of all nations are melted into a new race of men, whose labors and posterity will one day cause great changes in the world.

—Michel Guillaume Jean de Crevecoeur

153

But, in a larger sense, we cannot dedicate . . .
we cannot consecrate . . .
we cannot hallow this ground.
The brave men, living and dead, who struggled have
consecrated it, far above our poor power to add or detract.
The world will little note, nor long remember, what we say
here, but it can never forget what they did here.

—President Abraham Lincoln, Gettysburg Address

TODAY

GET UP AND SEE THE DAWN'S EARLY LIGHT!

Populism is folkish, patriotism is not.
One can be a patriot and a cosmopolitan.
But a populist is inevitably a nationalist of sorts.
Patriotism, too, is less racist than is populism.
A patriot will not exclude a person of another nationality
from the community where they have lived side by side
and whom he has known for many years,
but a populist will always remain suspicious
of someone who does not seem to belong to his tribe.

—John Lukacs

156

. . . It is a common observation here
that our cause is the cause of all mankind,
and that we are fighting for their liberty
in defending our own.

—Benjamin Franklin

Posterity—you will never know how much it has cost
my generation to preserve your freedom.
I hope you will make good use of it.

—President John Quincy Adams

TODAY

PRAY FOR YOUR COUNTRY!

The willingness with which our young people
are likely to serve in any war no matter how justified,
shall be directly proportional as to how they perceive
the veterans of earlier wars were treated
and appreciated by their nation.

—President George Washington

*Proclaim liberty throughout all the land
unto all the inhabitants thereof.*

—words written on the Liberty Bell

Liberty, when it begins to take root,
is a plant of rapid growth.

—President George Washington

TODAY

TAKE A KID TO SEE SOMETHING PATRIOTIC!

163

In the beginning of a change, the Patriot is a scarce man,
Brave, Hated, and Scorned.
When his cause succeeds however, the timid join him,
For then it costs nothing to be a patriot.

—Mark Twain

If one asks me the meaning of our flag, I say to him: It means all that the Constitution of our people, organizing for justice, for liberty, and for happiness, meant. Our flag carries American ideas, American history and American feelings. This American flag was the safeguard of liberty. It was an ordinance of liberty by the people, for the people. That it meant, that it means, and, by the blessing of God, that it shall mean to the end of time!

—Henry Ward Beecher

Patriotism is just loyalty to friends, people, families.

—Robert Santos

TODAY

SEE IF YOU COULD PASS
THE CITIZENSHIP TEST!

The inescapable price of liberty
is an ability to preserve it from destruction.

—General Douglas MacArthur

Off with your hat, as the flag goes by!
And let the heart have its say;
you're man enough for a tear in your eye
that you will not wipe away.

—Henry Cuyler Bunner

Everything that is really great and inspiring is created by individuals who labor in freedom.

—Albert Einstein

TODAY

FLY A FLAG!

This, then, is the state of the union:
free and restless, growing and full of hope.
So it was in the beginning.
So it shall always be, while God is willing,
and we are strong enough to keep the faith.

—President Lyndon B. Johnson

Whatever America hopes to bring to pass in the world must first come to pass in the heart of America.

—President Dwight D. Eisenhower

173

I hope to find my country in the right;
however, I will stand by her, right or wrong.

—John J. Crittenden

TODAY

HELP OUT A BOY OR GIRL SCOUT!

What we need are critical lovers of America—patriots
who express their faith in their country
by working to improve it.

—Hubert H. Humphrey

The first requisite of a good citizen in this republic of ours is
that he shall be able and willing to pull his own weight.

—President Theodore Roosevelt

We can't all be Washingtons, but we can all be patriots.

—Charles F. Browne

Our reliance is in the love of liberty . . .
Our defense is the spirit which prizes liberty
as the heritage of all men, in all lands everywhere.

—President Abraham Lincoln

TODAY

SIGN UP TO HELP BUILD A HABITAT FOR
HUMANITY HOUSE.
TELL JIMMY THAT CAROLE SENT YOU!

We know the best way to enhance freedom
in the other lands is to demonstrate here
that our democratic system is worthy of emulation.

—President Jimmy Carter

Ours is not only a fortunate people but a very common sensical people, with vision high but their feet on the earth, with belief in themselves and faith in God.

—President Warren G. Harding

Liberty without learning is always in peril
and learning without liberty is always in vain.

—President John F. Kennedy

There is no freedom on earth
or in any star
for those who deny freedom to others.

—Elbert Hubbard

184

TODAY

SAY SOMETHING WORTHY.

Peace and friendship with all mankind
is our wisest policy and I wish
we may be permitted to pursue it.

—President Thomas Jefferson

It is the love of country that has lighted and that keeps
glowing the holy fire of patriotism.

—J. Horace McFarland

America is a willingness of the heart.

—F. Scott Fitzgerald

America is not merely a nation, but a nation of nations.

—President Lyndon B. Johnson

There can be no greater good than the quest for peace, and no finer purpose than the preservation of freedom.

—President Ronald Reagan

TODAY

MAKE A DONATION TO A GOOD CAUSE!

The country's honor must be upheld at home and abroad.

—President Theodore Roosevelt

America is not a mere body of traders;
it is a body of free men. Our greatness is built upon
our freedom—is moral, not material.
We have a great ardor for gain;
but we have a deep passion for the rights of man.

—President Woodrow Wilson

My affections were first for my own country, and then,
generally, for all mankind.

—President Thomas Jefferson

TODAY

CALL YOUR MOM!

I contend that the strongest of all governments
is that which is most free.

–President William Henry Harrison

It is not the function of the government
to keep the citizen from falling into error;
it is the function of the citizen
to keep the government from falling into error.

—Robert H. Parker

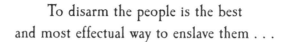

To disarm the people is the best
and most effectual way to enslave them . . .

—George Mason

TODAY

PRAY FOR A SOLDIER AND HIS OR HER FAMILY!

It is our duty still to endeavor to avoid war;
but if it shall actually take place, no matter by whom
brought on, we must defend ourselves.
If our house be on fire, without inquiring whether
it was fired from within or without,
we must try to extinguish it.

—President Thomas Jefferson

Three millions of people, armed in the holy cause of liberty,
and in such a country as that which we possess, are invincible
by any force which our enemy can send against us.

–Patrick Henry

The ultimate authority . . . resides in the people alone.

—President James Madison

The liberties of our country, the freedom of our civil Constitution, are worth defending at all hazards.

–Samuel Adams

Wherever the standard of freedom and independence
has been or shall be unfurled, there will be America's heart,
her benedictions and prayers, but she goes not abroad in
search of monsters to destroy. She is the well-wisher to the
freedom and independence of all. She is the champion and
vindicator of her own.

—President John Adams

204

TODAY

GIVE A HELPING HAND
TO SOMEONE WHO NEEDS IT!

The sacred rights of mankind are not to be rummaged for among old parchments or musty records. They are written, as with a sunbeam, in the whole volume of human nature by the hand of Divinity itself, and can never be erased or obscured by mortal power.

—Alexander Hamilton

I hope I shall always possess firmness and virtue enough to maintain what I consider the most enviable of all titles, the character of an honest man.

—President George Washington

Anywhere there are an oppressed people
who long for freedom and liberty,
I hope the flag of the United States is there.

—Douglas Doane

The advance of human freedom, the great achievement of our time, and the great hope of every time, now depends on us. Our nation, this generation, will lift a dark threat of violence from our people and our future. We will rally the world to this cause by our efforts, by our courage.

We will not tire, we will not falter, and we will not fail.

—President George W. Bush

TODAY

VOLUNTEER FOR SOMETHING, ANYTHING!

Victory at all costs, victory in spite of all terror,
victory however long and hard the road may be;
for without victory, there is no survival.

—Winston Churchill

Some people spend their whole lives wondering if
they made a difference.
The Marines don't have that problem.

—President Ronald Reagan

TODAY

BUY A PATRIOTIC BOOK
FOR YOUR LOCAL LIBRARY!

Human reason left to itself can neither preserve morals
nor give duration to a free government.

—Noah Webster

The meaning of America is not to be found in a life without toil. Freedom is not only bought with a great price; it is maintained by unremitting effort.

—President Calvin Coolidge

l or falter; we shall not weaken or tire . . .
he tools and we will finish the job.

—Winston Churchill

TODAY

MEMORIZE THE BILL OF RIGHTS!

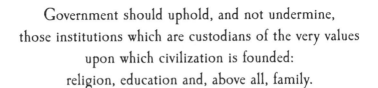

Government should uphold, and not undermine,
those institutions which are custodians of the very values
upon which civilization is founded:
religion, education and, above all, family.

—President Ronald Reagan

To educate a man in mind and not in morals is to educate a menace to society.

—President Theodore Roosevelt

The tree of liberty must be refreshed from time to time,
with the blood of patriots and tyrants.

—President Thomas Jefferson

My country owes me nothing.
It gave me, as it gives to every boy and girl, a chance.
It gave me schooling, independence of action,
opportunity for service and honor.
In no other land could a boy from a country village,
without inheritance or influential friends,
look forward with unbounded hope.

—President Herbert Hoover

221

TODAY

EXERCISE YOUR FREEDOM OF SPEECH . . .
BUT ONLY IN A POSITIVE WAY! (YES, ALL DAY!)

We will always remember.
We will always be proud.
We will always be prepared, so we may always be free.

—President Ronald Reagan

The difference between patriotism and nationalism is that the patriot is proud of his country for what it does, and the nationalist is proud of his country no matter what it does; the first attitude creates a feeling of responsibility, but the second a feeling of blind arrogance that leads to war.

—Sydney J. Harris

The God who gave us life,
gave us liberty at the same time:
the hand of force may destroy,
but cannot disjoin them.

—President Thomas Jefferson

You and I have a rendezvous with destiny. We will preserve for our children this, the last best hope of man on earth, or we will sentence them to take the first step into a thousand years of darkness. If we fail, at least let our children and our children's children say of us we justified our brief moment here. We did all that could be done.

—President Ronald Reagan

226

TODAY

READ A PATRIOTIC STORY
TO A KINDERGARTEN CLASS!

227

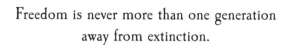

Freedom is never more than one generation
away from extinction.

—President Ronald Reagan

Let our object be our country, our whole country, and nothing but our country. And, by the blessing of God, may that country itself become a vast and splendid monument, not of oppression and terror, but of wisdom, of peace, and of liberty, upon which the world may gaze with admiration forever.

—Daniel Webster

It does not take a majority to prevail . . .
but rather an irate, tireless minority,
keen on setting brushfires of freedom in the minds of men.

−Samuel Adams

War has no certainty, except the certainty of sacrifice.

–President George W. Bush

What type of country would we be if we didn't defend the rights and freedoms of others, not because they're Americans, but how about just because they're human?

—Lonnie J. Lewis, Navy Corpsman

TODAY

SING YANKEE DOODLE DANDY—OUT LOUD!

A man who thinks of himself as belonging to a particular
national group in America has not yet become an American.

—President Woodrow Wilson

234

Every American takes pride in our tradition of hospitality to men of all races and all creeds. We must be constantly vigilant against the attacks of intolerance and injustice. We must scrupulously guard the civil rights and civil liberties of all citizens, whatever their background. We must remember that any oppression, any injustice, any hatred, is a wedge designed to attack our civilization.

—President Franklin D. Roosevelt

America is rising with a giant's strength.
Its bones are yet but cartilages.

—Fisher Ames

All our freedoms are a single bundle,
all must be secure if any is to be preserved.

—President Dwight D. Eisenhower

TODAY

SEND A CARD TO A VET!
OR SEND SIX CARDS TO SIX VETS!

Freedom is the sure possession of only those who have the courage to defend it.

—Anonymous

Especially important it is to realize that there can be no
assured peace and tranquility for any one nation except as it is
achieved for all. So long as want, frustration and a sense of
injustice prevail among significant sections of earth, no other
section can be wholly released from fear.

—President Dwight D. Eisenhower

Peace is the highest aspiration for the American people.
We will negotiate for it, sacrifice for it;
we will not surrender for it, now or ever.

—President Ronald Reagan

241

Men's hearts ought not be set against one another,
but set with one another, all against evil only.

—Thomas Carlyle

Patriotism depends as much on mutual suffering as on mutual success, and it is by that experience of all fortunes and all feelings that a great national character is created.

—Benjamin Disraeli

TODAY

DECORATE A GRAVESITE!

We must be ready to dare all for our country.
For history does not long entrust the care of freedom
to the weak or the timid.

−President Dwight D. Eisenhower

245

Of the many things we have done to democracy in the past,
the worst has been the indignity of taking it for granted.

—Max Lerner

This will remain the land of the free
only as long as it is the home of the brave.

—Elmer Davis

Those who won our independence believed liberty to be the secret of happiness and courage to be the secret of liberty.

—Louis D. Brandeis

TODAY

BUY SOME GROCERIES
FOR A HOMELESS FOOD PANTRY!

We need an America with the wisdom of experience.
But we must not let America grow old in spirit.

—Hubert H. Humphrey

Ours is the only country deliberately founded on a good idea.

—John Gunther

None who have always been free can understand
the terrible fascinating power of the hope of freedom
to those who are not free.

—Pearl S. Buck

252

We on this continent should never forget that men first crossed the Atlantic not to find soil for their ploughs but to secure liberty for their souls.

—Robert J. McCracken

TODAY

ASK GOD TO BLESS AMERICA!

If you take advantage of everything America has to offer,
there's nothing you can't accomplish.

—Geraldine Ferraro

In the truest sense, freedom cannot be bestowed;
it must be achieved.

—President Franklin D. Roosevelt

America is never wholly herself unless she is engaged in high moral principle. We as a people have such a purpose today.

—President George W. Bush

A free, virtuous, and enlightened people must know
full well the great principles and causes upon which
their happiness depends.

—President James Monroe

258

If you expect people to be ignorant and free you expect
what never was and never will be.

—President Thomas Jefferson

TODAY

DON'T MONDAY MORNING QUARTERBACK THE MILITARY!

Peace is a blessing, and like most blessings, it must be earned.

—President Dwight D. Eisenhower

Let the word go forth from this time and place, to friend and foe alike, that the torch has been passed to a new generation of Americans born in this century, tempered by war, disciplined by a hard and bitter peace.

—President John F. Kennedy

All battles are fought by scared men
who would have rather been somewhere else.

—John Wayne

Democracy is two wolves and a lamb voting on what to have
for lunch. Liberty is a well-armed lamb contesting the vote!

—Benjamin Franklin

To put the world right in order, we must first put the nation in order; to put the nation in order, we must first put the family in order; to put the family in order, we must first cultivate our personal life; we must first set our hearts right.

—Confucius

TODAY

PURSUE HAPPINESS!

Liberty lies in the hearts of men and women; when it dies there, no constitution, no law, no court can save it.

—Judge Learned Hand

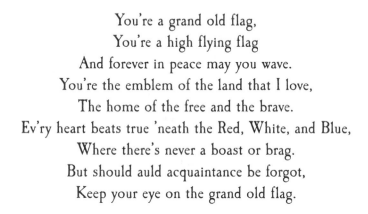

You're a grand old flag,
You're a high flying flag
And forever in peace may you wave.
You're the emblem of the land that I love,
The home of the free and the brave.
Ev'ry heart beats true 'neath the Red, White, and Blue,
Where there's never a boast or brag.
But should auld acquaintance be forgot,
Keep your eye on the grand old flag.

—George M. Cohan

Extremism in the defense of liberty is no vice.
Moderation in the pursuit of justice is no virtue.

—Senator Barry Goldwater

TODAY

REMEMBER WHEN YOU GO TO BED
THAT YOU'RE SLEEPING
IN THE BEST NATION ON EARTH!

The notion that a radical is one who hates his country is naive and usually idiotic. He is, more likely, one who likes his country more than the rest of us, and is thus more disturbed than the rest of us when he sees it debauched. He is not a bad citizen turning to crime; he is a good citizen driven to despair.

—H. L. Mencken

Moral cowardice that keeps us from speaking our minds is as dangerous to this country as irresponsible talk. The right way is not always the popular and easy way. Standing for right when it is unpopular is a true test of moral character.

—Margaret Chase Smith

A real patriot is the fellow who gets a parking ticket and
rejoices that the system works.

—Bill Vaughan

American history is longer, larger, more various,
more beautiful, and more terrible than anything
anyone has ever said about it.

—James Baldwin

TODAY

APPRECIATE DIVERSITY!

I look forward to a great future for America—
a future in which our country will match its military strength
with our moral restraint, its wealth with our wisdom,
its power with our purpose.

—President John F. Kennedy

We must always remember that America is a great nation
today not because of what government did for people but
because of what people did for themselves and for one another.

—President Richard Nixon

The things that will destroy America are prosperity-at-any-price, peace-at-any-price, safety-first instead of duty-first, the love of soft living and the get-rich-quick theory of life.

—President Theodore Roosevelt

In America, the photographer is not simply the person who records the past, but the one who invents it.

–Susan Sontag

TODAY

TAKE TIME TO LET A VET
SHARE A MEMORY WITH YOU!

280

It is by the goodness of God that in our country
we have those three unspeakably precious things:
freedom of speech, freedom of conscience, and the prudence
never to practice either of them.

—Mark Twain

The American people never carry an umbrella.
They prepare to walk in eternal sunshine.

—Alfred E. Smith

Americanism means the virtues of courage, honor,
justice, truth, sincerity, and hardihood—
the virtues that made America.

—President Theodore Roosevelt

283

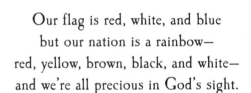

Our flag is red, white, and blue
but our nation is a rainbow—
red, yellow, brown, black, and white—
and we're all precious in God's sight.

—Rev. Jesse Jackson

TODAY

LEARN HOW TO FOLD
THE STAR-SPANGLED BANNER . . .
OR TEACH SOMEONE TO!

285

Our flag is our national ensign,
pure and simple, behold it!
Listen to it!
Every star has a tongue, every stripe is articulate.

—Former U.S. Senator Robert C. Winthrop

You can't appreciate home till you've left it, money till it's
spent, your wife until she's joined a woman's club, nor Old
Glory till you see her hanging on a broomstick on a shanty of
a consul in a foreign town.

—O. Henry

Let us talk sense to the American people.
Let us tell them the truth,
that there are not gains without pains.

—Theodor Wiesengrund

Whoever wants to know the heart and mind of America
had better learn baseball.

—Jacques Martin Barzun

289

This American system of ours . . .
call it Americanism, call it capitalism, call it what you like,
gives to each and every one of us a great opportunity if we only
seize it with both hands and make the most of it.

—Al Capone

America did not invent human rights.
In a very real sense . . . human rights invented America.

—President Jimmy Carter

There is nothing wrong with America that the faith, love of freedom, intelligence, and energy of her citizens can not cure.

—President Dwight D. Eisenhower

TODAY

LOOK UP THE MEANING OF
PATRIOTISM
IN THE DICTIONARY!

The infant, on opening his eyes,
ought to see his country,
and to the hour of his death never lose sight of it.

—Jean-Jacques Rousseau

He serves his party best, who serves the country best.

—President Rutherford B. Hayes

Such is the patriot's boast, where'er we roam
His first, best country is ever at home.

—Goldsmith

This is a maxim which I have received by hereditary tradition, not only from my father, but also from my grandfather and his ancestors, that after what I owe to God, nothing should be more dear or more sacred than the love and respect I owe to my country.

—De Thou

I love my country's good, with a respect more tender, more
holy and profound, than my own life.

—Shakespeare

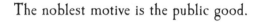

The noblest motive is the public good.

—Virgil

TODAY

THINK OF THREE THINGS
YOU ARE THANKFUL FOR!

The union of lakes, the union of lands,
The union of States none can sever,
The union of hearts, the union of hands,
And the flag of our Union forever!

—George P. Morris

How dear is fatherland to all noble hearts!

—Voltaire

The love of one's country is a splendid thing.
But why should love stop at the border?

—Pablo Casals

The love of country is the first virtue in a civilised man.

—Napoleon I

Patriotism itself is a necessary link in the golden chains
of our affections and virtues.

—Samuel Taylor Coleridge

305

I have heard something said about allegiance to the South.
I know no South, no North, no East, no West,
to which I owe any allegiance . . .
The Union, sir, is my country.

—Henry Clay, speech in the U.S. Senate

TODAY

BE SURE YOU KNOW THE NAME OF
THE PRESIDENT, VICE PRESIDENT, SECRETARY
OF STATE, SECRETARY OF DEFENSE, ETC.!

God has given you your country as cradle, and humanity as
mother; you cannot rightly love your brethren of the cradle if
you love not the common mother.

—Giuseppe Mazzini

Patriotism is in political life what faith is in religion.

—Lord Acton, *The Home and Foreign Review*

True patriotism sometimes requires of men to act exactly contrary, at one period, to that which it does at another, and the motive which impels them—the desire to do right—is precisely the same.

—General Robert E. Lee

I realize that patriotism is not enough.
I must have no hatred or bitterness towards anyone.

—Edith Cavell

The things that the flag stands for were created by the
experiences of a great people.
Everything that it stands for was written by their lives.
The flag is the embodiment, not of sentiment, but of history.

—President Woodrow Wilson

He who loves not his home and country which he has seen,
how shall he love humanity in general which he has not seen?

—William Ralph Inge

TODAY

WRITE YOUR OWN PATRIOTIC QUOTATION!

We will survive and become the stronger—not only because of a patriotism that stands for love of country, but a patriotism that stands for a love of people.

—President Gerald R. Ford

The person who wants to fight senses his solitude and is frightened. Whereupon the silence reverts to patriotism. Fear finds its great moral revelation in patriotism.

—Jacobo Timerman,
Prisoner Without a Name, Cell Without a Number

I think there is one higher office than president,
and I would call that patriot.

—Former U.S. Senator Gary Hart

The worth of a State, in the long run,
is the worth of the individuals composing it.

—John Stuart Mill

There comes a time when it is good for a nation to know
that it must sacrifice if need be everything that it has to
vindicate the principles which it possesses.

—President Woodrow Wilson

All nations have present, or past, or future reasons
for thinking themselves incomparable.

—Paul Valery

Would the honest patriot, in full tide of successful experiment, abandon a government which has so far kept us free and firm?

—President Thomas Jefferson

In time of war the loudest patriots are the greatest profiteers.

—August Bebel

I love the Americans because they love liberty.

—William Pitt

TODAY

THANK GOD FOR DEMOCRACY!

324

We do not profess to be the champions of liberty, and then
consent to see liberty destroyed.

—President Woodrow Wilson

God grants liberty only to those who love it, and are always
ready to guard and defend it.

—Daniel Webster

Liberty relies upon itself,
invites no one,
promises nothing,
sits in calmness and light,
is positive and composed,
and knows no discouragement.

—Walt Whitman, *Leaves of Grass*

Liberty is the means in the pursuit of happiness.

—President William H. Taft

328

Liberty is the bread of man's spirit.

—Salvador de Madariaga

That country is the richest which nourishes the greatest
number of noble and happy human beings.

—John Ruskin

TODAY

THANK GOD FOR FREEDOM!

When an American says that he loves his country, he . . .
means that he loves an inner air,
an inner light in which freedom lives
and in which a man can draw the breath of self-respect.

—Adlai Stevenson

You cannot conquer America.

—William Pitt

Our true nationality is mankind.

—H. G. Wells

The first requisite of a good citizen in this republic of ours is that he shall be able and willing to pull his weight.

—President Theodore Roosevelt

335

The true test of civilization is not the census,
nor the size of cities, nor the crops—
no, but the kind of man the country turns out.

—Ralph Waldo Emerson

However distinguished by rank or property,
in the rights of freedom we are all equal.

—Junius, *Public Advertiser*

TODAY

WEAR SOMETHING PATRIOTIC TO WORK,
JUST BECAUSE!

If a nation values anything more than freedom, it will lose its freedom; and the irony of it is that if it is comfort or money that it values more, it will lose that too.

—W. Somerset Maugham, *Strictly Personal*

Freedom belongs to the strong.

—Richard Wright, *Long Black Song*

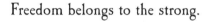

Citizens are not born, but made.

—Baruch Spinoza, *Tractatus Politicus*

It is not the function of our Government to keep the citizen from falling into error; it is the function of the citizen to keep the Government from falling into error.

—Robert H. Jackson, *American Communications Association*

Politics ought to be the part-time profession of every citizen
who would protect the rights and privileges of free people
and who would preserve what is good and fruitful
in our national heritage.

—President Dwight D. Eisenhower

343

Democracy arises out of the notion
that those who are equal in any respect
are equal in all respects;
because men are equally free,
they claim to be absolutely equal.

—Aristotle

TODAY

SING AMERICA THE BEAUTIFUL
OUT LOUD IN THE SHOWER!

345

The foundation on which all our constitutions are built is the natural equality of men.

—President Thomas Jefferson

There can be no truer principle than this—that every individual of the community at large has an equal right to the protection of government.

—Alexander Hamilton

Equality—the informing soul of Freedom!

—President James A. Garfield, *Maxims*

348

It is harder to preserve than to obtain liberty.

—Vice President John C. Calhoun

The liberty of the individual is the greatest thing of all,
it is on this and on this alone
that the true will of the people can develop.

—Alexander Ivanovich Herzen

Eternal vigilance is the price of liberty.

—Wendell Phillips

I want every American to stand up for his rights,
even if he has to sit down for them.

—President John F. Kennedy

You have to love a nation that celebrates its independence
every July 4, not with a parade of guns, tanks, and soldiers who
file by the White House in a show of strength and muscle, but
with family picnics where kids throw frisbees, the potato salad
gets iffy, and the flies die from happiness.
You may think you have overeaten, but it is patriotism.

—Erma Bombeck

353

TODAY

WATCH AN OLD PATRIOTIC MOVIE;
IT'S OK TO CRY!

If there is a better country than America—GO TO IT!

—Nick Snider, Founder, National Museum of Patriotism,
Atlanta, Georgia

I ask you to join in a re-United States. We need to empower our people so they can take more responsibility for their own lives in a world that is ever smaller, where everyone counts. We need a new spirit of community, a sense that we are all in this together, or the American Dream will continue to wither. Our destiny is bound up with the destiny of every other American.

—President William Jefferson Clinton

To me, patriotism is the plumber tackling the stopped-up toilet, the homemaker building a casserole out of leftovers, the teacher listening to a slow reader read . . . . a . . . . book . . . . like . . . . this. It's the garbage man—all hail to him! And the gardener weeding on his knees. And the security guard on lonely night duty. Everyone who makes America go-round a little better every day is a patriot. What better way to serve your country than where you stand, doing what you do?

—Carole Marsh, author and publisher/founder,
Gallopade International

Americanism is a question of principle,
of purpose, of idealism, or character;
it is not a matter of birthplace or creed or line of descent."

—President Theodore Roosevelt

If we cannot end now our differences, at least we can help
make the world safe for diversity.

—President John F. Kennedy

The future doesn't belong to the faint-hearted.
It belongs to the brave.

—President Ronald Reagan

TODAY

PLAN THE BEST FOURTH OF JULY
EVER FOR THE COMING YEAR!

America is best described by one word—freedom.

—President Dwight D. Eisenhower, 1958

America is successful because of the hard work,
and creativity, and enterprise of our people.

—President George W. Bush

We will not forget that Liberty has here made her home;
nor shall her chosen altar be neglected.

—President Grover Cleveland

I Pledge Allegiance to the flag
of the United States of America
and to the Republic for which it stands,
one Nation under God, indivisible,
with liberty and justice for all.

—Francis Bellamy, The Pledge of Allegiance

More Patriotic Titles by Carole Marsh:

- *Pa • tri • ot • isms* (companion to *The Daily Patriot*)

- Patriotic Favorites Coloring and Activity Book
- Young Patriot's Book of Puzzles, Games, Riddles, Stories, Poems, and Activities

- My American Flag to Color and Display! Activity Pack
- The Pledge of Allegiance Activity Pack
- America the Beautiful Activity
- The Star Spangled Banner Activity Pack

- The White House Christmas Mystery